KRIS BRYANT

Jon M. Fishman

Lerner Publications ◆ Minneapolis

Lerner Publications Company
A division of Lerner Publishing Group, Inc.
241 First Avenue North
Minneapolis, MN 55401 USA

For reading levels and more information, look up this title at www.lernerbooks.com.

Main body text set in Albany Std 15/22. Typeface provided by Agfa.

Library of Congress Cataloging-in-Publication Data

Names: Fishman, Jon M., author.
Title: Kris Bryant / by Jon M. Fishman.
Description: Minneapolis, Minnesota : Lerner Publications, [2018] | Series: Sports
    All-Stars | Includes bibliographical references and index. | Audience: Ages: 7–11. |
    Audience: Grades: 4 to 6.
Identifiers: LCCN 2017029265| ISBN 9781512482461 (lb) | ISBN 9781541512047
    (pb) | ISBN 9781512482621 (eb pdf)
Subjects: LCSH: Bryant, Kris, 1992– —Juvenile literature. | Baseball players—United
    States—Biography—Juvenile literature. | Chicago Cubs (Baseball team)—
    History—Juvenile literature.
Classification: LCC GV865.B89 F57 2018 | DDC 796.357092 [B] —dc23

LC record available at https://lccn.loc.gov/2017029265

Manufactured in the United States of America
1-43295-33115-9/20/2017

CONTENTS

BREAKING THE
CURSE

Kris Bryant takes off after smashing a hit during Game 7 of the 2016 World Series.

Chicago Cubs third baseman Kris Bryant stepped to home plate. He dug into the dirt with his **cleats**. It was Game 7 of the 2016 World Series. The Cubs and the Cleveland Indians had each won three games in the series. It all came down to Game 7. Baseball's championship was on the line.

Bryant's knees were bent. He held the bat high near his head as the pitcher threw the baseball. *Crack!* Bryant swung and sent the ball streaking to the outfield for a base hit. He scored when a teammate smacked another hit. That gave the Cubs the lead, 2–1.

Some Cubs fans believed the team was cursed before they won the 2016 World Series. At a game in 1945, fan William Sianis tried to bring his pet goat to the ballpark. When he was turned away, Sianis said, "Them Cubs, they ain't gonna win no more."

Playing in the World Series is the goal for every Major League Baseball (MLB) team. It was even more special for the Cubs. They were playing with 108 years of history and drama behind them. The team had last won the World Series in 1908. It was by far the longest streak without a championship in MLB. Some fans thought the Cubs would never win the World Series again.

Bryant next came to bat in the following inning. This time, he drew a **base on balls** and later scored. Bryant's second run put the Cubs ahead 5–1.

Cleveland kept fighting. Down by three runs in the eighth inning, the Indians came roaring back. They tied the game, 6–6. Then neither team scored in the ninth.

That meant Game 7 would go to extra innings for just the fourth time in World Series history.

Before the 10th inning began, rain started pelting the field. Fans and players took shelter. The game was delayed for 17 minutes.

Tension filled the stadium in the 10th inning. The Cubs belted three hits and scored two runs to take the lead. But Cleveland had shown that they wouldn't give up. A base on balls and a hit made the score Chicago 8, Cleveland 7. The Indians were down to their final out.

Bryant (right) scores a run during Game 7 against Cleveland.

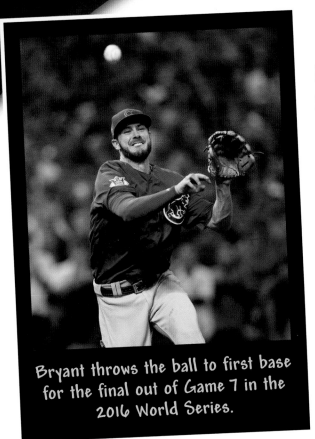

Bryant throws the ball to first base for the final out of Game 7 in the 2016 World Series.

Cleveland second baseman Michael Martinez was up next. He swung and sent the ball bouncing slowly along the ground. Bryant charged forward. He knew he had to hurry. He bent down, snatched the ball with his bare hand, and fired it to first base. Out! The Cubs were World Series champions!

Baseball fans everywhere were happy for Chicago. President Barack Obama had lived in the city and rooted for the Chicago White Sox. But even he was thrilled with the Cubs' win. "It happened: Cubs win World Series," he wrote on Twitter. "Want to come to the White House?"

Bryant (right) celebrates with his teammates after the Cubs win the 2016 World Series.

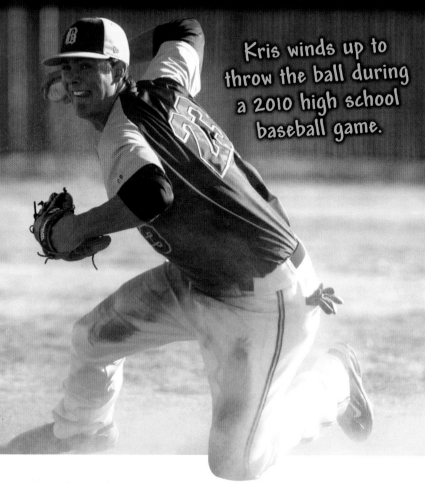

Kris winds up to throw the ball during a 2010 high school baseball game.

Kris Bryant was born on January 4, 1992, in Las Vegas, Nevada. He lived there with his parents and his older brother, Nick. His father, Mike Bryant, had been a baseball player. The Boston Red Sox chose him in the 1980 MLB **draft**.

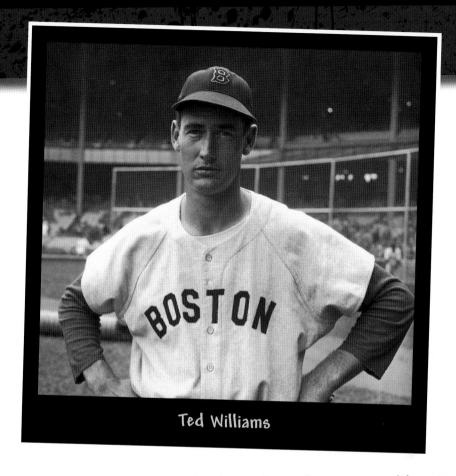

Ted Williams

He played two seasons in the **minor leagues** without much success. He ended his career with a poor .204 **batting average**. But he passed his love of the sport to his son.

Mike Bryant had learned a lot about baseball during his playing days. He worked on batting with Red Sox legend Ted Williams. Many fans think of Williams as the greatest hitter ever. Mike Bryant told Kris, "I'm going to teach you to hit like Ted Williams."

Kris's father gave hitting lessons to local kids in a **batting cage** behind the Bryant home. When he was five years old, Kris began hitting in the cage too. His father gave him pointers he'd learned from Williams. The lessons paid off. Kris hit his first home run in a game when he was eight. His father picked him up and hugged him as Kris ran past third base.

His father sold his furniture business around the time of Kris's first home run. He took a job with steadier hours so he could always be at Kris's games. He also had more time for lessons in the backyard batting cage. He used photos of Ted Williams to inspire and teach his son.

Kris hit 25 home runs in his first three years of high school.

Kris poses for a photo as a high school player for the Bonanza High School Bengals.

By his senior season, he had become a genuine **slugger**. He smashed 22 home runs that year alone. He was good enough to earn a **scholarship** to the University of San Diego.

Bryant continued to grow as a player at San Diego. In 2013, he crushed 31 home runs. The baseball website *Baseball America* named him its College Player of the Year. Then, in June, the Cubs chose Bryant with the second overall pick in the MLB draft.

Bryant stands at bat during a 2013 college baseball game in San Diego.

Bryant puts on his new Cubs jersey
after the 2013 draft.

Growing up in Nevada, Bryant hadn't been a Cubs fan. He didn't know much about the team. "I know they haven't won a World Series in a while," he said. "Hopefully I can do all that I can to help the Cubs win one."

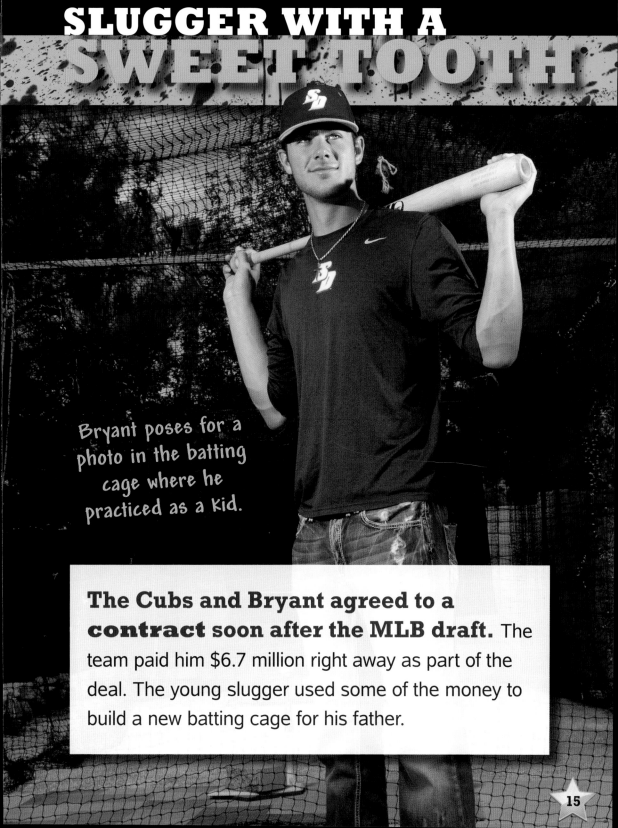

SLUGGER WITH A SWEET TOOTH

Bryant poses for a photo in the batting cage where he practiced as a kid.

The Cubs and Bryant agreed to a contract soon after the MLB draft. The team paid him $6.7 million right away as part of the deal. The young slugger used some of the money to build a new batting cage for his father.

Bryant's father sits in the batting cage at
his home in Las Vegas.

The batting cage in Las Vegas is 65 feet (20 m) long
and 15 feet (4.6 m) high. Bryant still practices there often.
The cage has heavy-duty netting to catch the balls he
smashes. He may start his workouts by hitting balls
from a **tee**. Then he turns on the pitching machine. The
machine can throw balls at many different speeds and
angles. Bryant turns it up to 96 miles (154 km) per hour.
"I make sure it's tough on me," he said.

Bryant stays fit in other ways when he isn't playing baseball or crushing balls in the batting cage. He spends the MLB **off-season** in Las Vegas. But chances are Bryant won't be there if you stop by his home. He might be out running in his neighborhood. He thinks the winter weather in Las Vegas is perfect for long runs. He also lifts weights and exercises at the gym.

After a workout, it's time to eat. Bryant knows he needs healthful food to build his muscles and heal after a tough day in the batting cage. **Protein** is especially important. He eats protein-heavy foods such as meat and beans. He even drinks shakes rich in protein to make sure he gets enough.

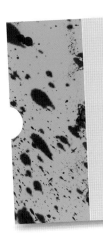

Bryant says he wouldn't want to train without listening to music. He listens to many different kinds of music. He especially likes hearing new artists and songs.

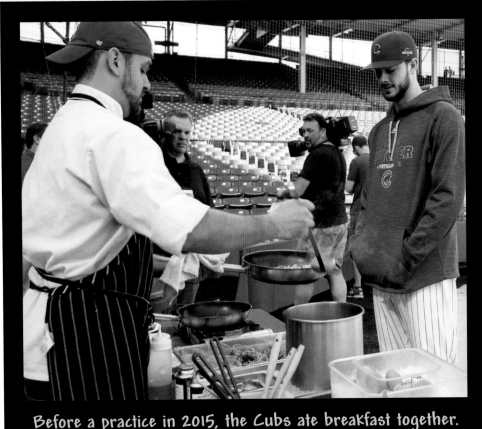

Before a practice in 2015, the Cubs ate breakfast together. The team chef prepared plenty of healthful food for the team.

While Bryant knows how important healthful food is, he also believes it's important to let loose sometimes and eat whatever you want. He loves hot dogs. He gets lots of candy when he goes to movies. And one of his favorite snacks is ice cream. Someone once asked him if he preferred ice cream or cake. Bryant said, "Ice cream with cake."

EASYGOING
SUPERSTAR

Bryant and his wife, Jessica, attend an event in Chicago.

In 2006, Kris Bryant met Jessica Delp in a high school English class. The couple got married about two months after the Cubs won the 2016 World Series. They lead a low-key lifestyle even though Kris is one of the most popular sports stars in Chicago.

Jessica Delp and Bryant watch a basketball game in Las Vegas in 2015.

After games, Bryant spends a few hours relaxing at home. He hangs out on the couch, watching TV and eating ice cream. He thinks this time is important to calm himself and reduce stress. Bryant and his wife spend a lot of time watching movies and taking it easy.

They also love to explore new restaurants. And Chicago has a lot of them! Bryant especially likes steak houses. There's always a new place to try in the city. In fact, Bryant says the only things he doesn't like about Chicago are the potholes in the streets.

At home Bryant usually wears jeans and T-shirts. But fans are used to seeing a more fashionable side of the slugger. He models for the clothing company Express.

A billboard outside Wrigley Field, where the Cubs play, displays an Express ad featuring Bryant.

Photos of him wearing Express's clothes appear in magazines and on social media. Fans may even see him on huge billboards all around Chicago. He does ads for other companies as well, such as Red Bull.

Bryant's status as a celebrity helps him to give back to his community. He hosts charity poker and golf tournaments in the Las Vegas area. The events raise money for children in need and much more. Bryant says the tournaments are great ways to help people—plus he gets to have fun playing golf and poker!

Home Run Derby

MLB holds a Home Run Derby contest each year before the All-Star Game. People throw easy pitches to the game's best hitters to see who can hit the most home runs. In 2015, Bryant took part in the derby. He got to choose who would pitch to him. He picked the man who had thrown to him for as long as he could remember—his father.

Bryant didn't hit enough home runs to win the derby. But he and his dad had a great time anyway. Bryant gave his dad a big hug when it was over. "That was awesome!" Bryant said.

Bryant hugs his dad at the end of the Home Run Derby.

INSTANT IMPACT

Bryant played in 68 games with the Tennessee Smokies in 2014.

Like his father, Kris Bryant started his pro career in the minor leagues. In 2013, Bryant played for four minor-league teams and hit 15 home runs. The next season, he played for two teams. His .325 batting average and 43 home runs proved that he was ready for MLB.

Bryant plays a game with the Iowa Cubs in 2015.

Still, the Cubs hesitated. Bryant began the 2015 season in the minor leagues. Some fans were upset. They thought the team was just trying to save money. The more time a player spends in the major leagues, the more a team may have to pay him later. The Cubs could save money in the future by delaying the start of Bryant's major-league career.

Bryant played just seven minor-league games in 2015. He played his first major-league game with the

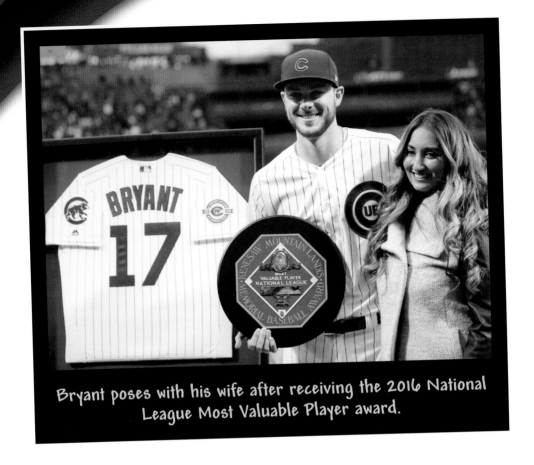

Bryant poses with his wife after receiving the 2016 National League Most Valuable Player award.

Cubs in April. And he made a huge impact on the team. That season he smashed 26 home runs and won the National League (NL) **Rookie** of the Year award. In 2016, he crushed 39 home runs and was voted NL Most Valuable Player. And he helped the Cubs win the World Series for the first time in 108 years.

Bryant had become a Chicago legend in just two seasons with the team. It would be easy for him to feel satisfied with what he had achieved. But Bryant's goal is to keep working and getting better. "I get told so much, 'You've had such a good career in your first two years, what are you going to do?'" Bryant said. "I just want to continue to improve."

Bryant celebrates winning the World Series in 2016.

All-Star Stats

The **Chicago Cubs** have been around longer than most **MLB** teams. In more than 100 years, only nine **Cubs** players have hit more home runs than Bryant did in 2016. Take a look at where he ranks on **Chicago's** all-time home run list for a season.

Player	Home Runs (Season)
Sammy Sosa	66 (1998)
Sammy Sosa	64 (2001)
Sammy Sosa	63 (1999)
Hack Wilson	56 (1930)
Sammy Sosa	50 (2000)
Andre Dawson	49 (1987)
Sammy Sosa	49 (2002)
Dave Kingman	48 (1979)
Ernie Banks	47 (1958)
Derrek Lee	46 (2005)
Ernie Banks	45 (1959)
Ernie Banks	44 (1955)
Ernie Banks	43 (1957)
Billy Williams	42 (1970)
Ernie Banks	41 (1960)
Hank Sauer	41 (1954)
Ryne Sandberg	40 (1990)
Sammy Sosa	40 (2003)
Sammy Sosa	40 (1996)
Moises Alou	39 (2004)
Kris Bryant	39 (2016)
Rogers Hornsby	39 (1929)
Hack Wilson	39 (1929)

Source Notes

6 Associated Press, "Cubs Outlast Indians in Game 7, Win First World Series Since 1908," *ESPN*, November 3, 2016, http://www.espn.com/mlb/recap?gameId=361102105.

8 Ibid.

11 Tom Verducci, "Born to Win: Is the Kris Bryant Story Too Good to Be True? No, but the Cubs Will Take It," *Sports Illustrated*, March 21, 2017, https://www.si.com/mlb/2017/03/21/kris-bryant-chicago-cubs-born-win.

14 Jesse Rogers, "Rapid Reaction: Cubs Draft 3B Bryant," *ESPN*, June 7, 2013, http://www.espn.com/blog/chicago/cubs/post/_/id/17474/rapid-reaction-cubs-draft-3b-bryant.

16 Tom Verducci, "Bryant on Bryant: Cubs' Superstar Opens Up about Life at the Plate and off the Field," *Sports Illustrated*, March 22, 2017, https://www.si.com/mlb/2017/03/22/kris-bryant-interview-chicago-cubs.

18 Josh Noel, "Kris Bryant Dishes on Life outside of Baseball," *Chicago Tribune*, May 24, 2016, http://www.chicagotribune.com/lifestyles/magazine/ct-mag-summer-2016-kris-bryant-20160506-story.html.

23 Blair Sheade, "Kris Bryant and His Dad Shared a Special Moment at Home Run Derby," *Chicago Sun Times*, June 24, 2016, http://chicago.suntimes.com/sports/kris-bryant-and-his-dad-shared-a-special-moment-at-home-run-derby.

27 Verducci, "Bryant on Bryant."

Glossary

base on balls: four pitches outside of the strike zone that allow a batter to take first base. A base on balls is also called a walk.

batting average: the ratio of a batter's hits per times at bat

batting cage: an enclosed space for batting practice

cleats: shoes with spikes on the bottom that baseball players wear

contract: an agreement between an athlete and a team that determines a player's salary and time with the team

draft: an event in which teams take turns choosing new players

minor leagues: baseball leagues where players train and hope to move up to Major League Baseball

off-season: the part of the year when a sports league is not playing

protein: a substance in food that the body needs

rookie: a first-year player

scholarship: money to help pay for college

slugger: a player who hits a lot of home runs

tee: a post on which a ball is placed

Braun, Eric. *Super Baseball Infographics*. Minneapolis: Lerner Publications, 2015.

Gitlin, Marty. *Kris Bryant: Baseball Star*. Lake Elmo, MN: Focus Readers, 2017.

Kris Bryant
http://m.mlb.com/player/592178/kris-bryant

MLB
http://www.mlb.com/mlb/kids

Official Site of the Chicago Cubs
https://www.mlb.com/cubs

Savage, Jeff. *Baseball Super Stats*. Minneapolis: Lerner Publications, 2018.

Index

Photo Acknowledgments

The images in this book are used with the permission of: iStock.com/63151 (gold and silver stars); Michael Hickey/Getty Images, p. 2; Nick Cammett/Diamond Images/ Getty Images, pp. 4–5; Ezra Shaw/Getty Images, pp. 7, 9, 27; Brad Mangin/MLB Photos/Getty Images, p. 8; © Josh Holmberg/Icon SMI, pp. 10, 12; Bettmann/Getty Images, p. 11; AP Photo/Lenny Ignelzi, p. 13; AP Photo/Charles Rex Arbogast, p. 14; Nelvin C. Cepeda/ZUMA Press/Newscom, p. 15; AP Photo/John Locher, p. 16; AP Photo/Nam Y. Huh, p. 18; Tasos Katopodis/Getty Images, p. 19; Ethan Miller/Getty Images, p. 20; Joe Robbins/Getty Images, p. 21; Brace Hemmelgarn/Minnesota Twins/Getty Images, p. 23; AP Photo/Tony Farlow/Four Seam, p. 24; Stephen Lew/ Icon Sportswire/Getty Images, p. 25; AP Photo/Charles Rex Arbogast, p. 26.

Front cover: Michael Hickey/Getty Images; iStock.com/neyro2008.